Phenomena

Frank Dux

For dear Anita,

Frank Dux

Published in 2011 by Antony Rowe Publishing
48-50 Birch Close
Eastbourne
East Sussex
BN23 6PE
arp@cpi-group.co.uk

A catalogue record for this book is available from the British Library

ISBN 978-1-907571-06-0

Printed and Bound in Great Britain by
CPI Antony Rowe, Chippenham and Eastbourne

FSC
Mixed Sources
Product group from well-managed
forests and other controlled sources
Cert no. SGS-COC-2953
www.fsc.org
© 1996 Forest Stewardship Council

Contents

Acknowledgements

Some of these poems have appeared elsewhere:

"The Dart at Sharpham" in *Outposts*

"The Annunciation" in *The Paris Review*

"The Luohan", "The Shadow", "A Cruel Winter", "Lunch
in Kardamyli", "The Moon & Mars in Mani", "Eight for
Dinner" & "My Un-named Horror" in *Acumen*

"Phenomena" & "Storm at Sea" in *Poetry News*

"Trees" & "Taygetos I" in *Agenda*

"Somatianá" (entitled "Snake") in *Manifest*

"Coming Down to Drink" was commended in the *National Poetry
Competition*

Readers may recognise the following lines from other poets' works:

Page 7: "Is written down in rings of grain" is incorporated from
Philip Larkin's "The Trees", as an act of homage really.

Page 14: "and quiring angels . . . praise of God" is a gloss on T.
S. Eliot's similar lines in "The Hippopotamus". There are
also several borrowings here from the King James version of
The Bible.

Page 69: "For know there are three worlds . . ." is an echo from
Shelley in "Prometheus Unbound".

Page 71: Some lines, or parts thereof, are similar to the
comparable ones in William Congreve's translation of the
Tenth Book of Ovid's Metamorphoses.

There are also a few lines from Shakespeare here and there
throughout the book

This collection owes much to the enthusiasm shown by friends
and others to whom I have over time spoken many of these
poems. Special thanks are due to George Scanlon for his
consistently astute and learned comments, to Anne Boston
for her sensible suggestions as she cast her expert eye over the
typescript, and of course to Margarita of Somatianá.

The Poems

Phenomena

Phenomena in poise
Contain what will be done:
The statue in the stone,
The music in the noise.

All that time affords,
All that's yet to be:
The coffin in the tree,
The poem in the words.

Coming down to drink

What beasts are these coming down to drink
at the shallow pools in the river bed?
The drought has drawn them out.
                              And now the herdsmen;
two, three. One squats; the others stand leaning
on their spears. They do not watch the herd.
Their eyes rest in space. A breeze rises, stirs
the grass — and memory. Where have I seen
these men before? and these elegant beasts
with outswept horns?
                              The squatting man now stands.
The herd is clambering back up the bank,
dry clods breaking away under their hooves.
This too is memory — as is the rain,
large drops at first, spattering the dust,
a sudden coolness falling on my arms.

I hear a rush of sound

I hear a rush of sound blow through the wood.
The wind is tempting all the trees to move,
the green, the gaunt, the living and the dead,
swaying to the wild whispering of love.
I listen closely to their swish and creak,
the supple living ones, the brittle ghosts.
I am familiar with the dead who speak,
mingling their voices with their living hosts,
roots sharing still the dark, sustaining earth,
disintegrating to become that earth.
These whispers are as when I first awoke,
with visions heard, seeing without sight.
Through me they move and speak; they even write
upon the trembling leaves of this my book.

You Meet Someone

You meet someone, exchange some words somewhere
when suddenly somehow you are aware
this person met is actually a god —
or — you see in the distance something odd
perhaps, an object or creature of some kind.
You don't know what. You approach it and you find
usually it's just a trick of light
or something juxtaposed, or a slight
and common thing, utterly common. But
this time when your perceptions are acute
you see something unearthly has been bared.
So — the question is: are you prepared?
Keep watch: the distinction is so small.
It has been said: the readiness is all.

The Dart at Sharpham

Low water, slack, at dusk; the river's bend
between the reeds gone russet and the hill
beyond, from where a tractor's roar of toil
does not disturb the hush that here is found,
which is a presence, not a lack of sound.

A pair of swans, one the other leading;
a crying of gulls out on the tidal flat;
a heron upstream, low, the long wing beat;
and here a corpse: a riverboat corroding,
the dead weight of mud its present loading.

And here is peace for me, a gift unwon,
and willingness to die if I die here
enclosed within this open bowl, no fear;
the settled plenitude of life keeps on
with dark and light and the cycles of the moon.

Trees

Those trees that occupy the ridge
And lean to the prevailing wind;
The dark complexity of mind
Within this ancient growth of hedge;
The seven brawny sycamores
That stand as guardians in a row
Beside the lonely hill farm, though
The house is empty and the doors
Broke in; the apple trees I'm told
I should cut down before the spring
To stop the spread of cankering:
These are the witnesses; they hold
The evidence and know the law.
The giant pachydermous beech,
The corrugated oak, they each
May fall to rot, to storm or saw,
Or stand until their time runs down.
But in their living dying being
There is an unrelenting seeing
Through every pore from root to crown.

Stones have been known to move and trees to speak.
I wait and watch within when branches creak.
And I have heard the whispers in the wood,
The singing in the sap which is their blood;
And on the wind-blown ridge I've listened for
The secret opening of their secret door.

These are the trees who see each thing
Before it parts from everything,
Who see the act before the act
Divides and is defined as fact.
The moon gives off reflected light,
The sun as seen in second sight.
The moon and sun are seen as one:
There is no moon, there is no sun.
These are the seers without eyes
Who see the day that never dies.
What's dark is light, what's small's immense,
The slow is quick, the jagged plain;

A radiant circumambience
Is written down in rings of grain,
But only can be read in slices,
And is at best a partial view.
You must listen for the voices.
Take in their breath that passes through
The borders of the other senses.
You'll hear the turning of the keys,
The easing open of defences,
And then you'll hear along with these
The speaking and the singing of the trees.

The Cutting Edge

I write this at the cutting edge of time
where every now is killed off as it's born,
so that what is already was, the sum
of being is subtracted, what we earn
through time impounded by that time at source.
Nothing to hold; to be is not to be.
And yet — there seems a cunning or a force,
that as we die in time we still can be.

Complete existence is as music played:
to give time to the next each note must die,
for of successive deaths is music made
and held suspended, live, in memory.
The mighty giver-taker, lord of all,
is music-master god, total recall.

Hamlet

From time to time the grievous thought uprears,
that all I do is by one fatal flaw
undone, condemned by unremitting law,
corruption rules all moments, days, all years.
All without hope. But see act one scene four:
"So, oft it chances in particular men."
"So, oft"! So there's my balm, my oxygen:
communion teaching patience to endure.
I'm not alone in suffering this pain.
Yet — stays the poison buried at the core;
corruption shared is yet corrupt no less.
But why am I so special to complain?
Have I not borne this "dram of eale", this sore,
this wound, and made of it my life's finesse?

Brixton Water Lane

That summer evening in the garden
when each distinct successive moment
went rushing one upon the other:
the boy moving, seen through the window;
the woman in the chair talking.
I sat, timeless, witnessing time,
in open wonder, uninvolved.
And I could stay there if I wished,
the staying and the wishing
sustained in perfect balance.

Then — when? — later I came back
to where I was, but now immersed,
fallen from the balance
into the stream of time.

I try now to relive, to bring back
those moments witnessed in eternity:
the boy, his movement as he crossed the room,
the woman to my left, the clarity
of vision, and my state, so intimate
yet foreign to my ordinary life,
where now I struggle to regain the poise
I lost, and can't remember how or when.
A roaring current carries me away,
time's one-time witness drowned in time.

Founex, Lac Léman

Great grey clouds are sweeping across the sky
above the fluttering poplars, heavy, yet
propelled with urgent power, like dark regret
smothering the early hints of day.
If I were to another era born,
I'd cry a question to those harbingers:
What dooms, what demolitions, what massacres
are prologued by this shrouding of the dawn?

But nature now provides no auguries.
Cloud and wind are atmospheric facts,
no more. Why, then, this deadening unease,
as if before impending monstrous acts?
as if I hear the roar of righteousness
and laughter at our decent helplessness.

Armageddon

And when the thousand years are expired,
Satan shall be loosed out of his prison,
and shall go out to deceive the nations
(which are in the four quarters of the earth),
Gog and Magog, to gather them together
to battle. The machines of war shall meet
upon the place which in the Hebrew tongue
is called Armageddon.
                          It shall be seen
that in the air above them and underneath
the earth, where on the pavements of the cities,
the squares and markets, the alley-ways, the dark
and secret places, all shall groan and tremble.
And there shall fall upon them a great hail
out of heaven, with thunders and lightnings.
And when the nations, the people thereof
(which are in the four quarters of the earth),
shall see these things, many shall be afraid,
but others among them shall shout for joy.
And on their screens, whereon their eyes are fixed,
an angel shall they see come down from heaven,
having great power; and the earth is lightened
with his glory; and mightily he cries
with a strong voice: "Babylon the great
is fallen, is fallen, that was the habitation
of devils and the hold of foul spirits."
Then a great white throne shall they see, and him
that sitteth on it, from whose face the earth
and heaven flee away, and there is found no place
for them. And on their screens they see the dead,
small and great, standing before God;
and the books are opened, and another book
is opened, which is the book of life;
and the dead are judged out of those things
which are written in the books, according to
their works. Even the sea gives up its dead,
and all places are delivered of them.
And when the nations, the people thereof
(which are in the four quarters of the earth),
behold these things shown on the news reports,

with wonder and with worry they will cry out
as with one voice: "The judgment day has come."
And they shall see the new Jerusalem,
the holy city, coming down from God
out of heaven, prepared as a bride
adorned for her husband, and a great voice
out of heaven saying: "Behold,
the tabernacle of God is with his people,
and God himself shall be with them and be their God,
and God shall wipe away all tears,
and there shall be no more death,
neither sorrow nor crying,
neither shall there be any more pain,
for the former things are passed away."
And he that sitteth on the throne shall say:
"Behold, I make all things new! I am
the Alpha and Omega, the beginning and the end."
And when the nations, the people thereof
(which are in the four quarters of the earth),
shall hear and view these things upon their screens —
for all the channels, terrestrial and sky,
have sent their crews to cover these events,
both male and female, many of great courage —
the people shall be fearful and desperate
and cry out: "See, the judgment is upon them,
and not upon us, and we shall not be taken
into the new Jerusalem."
And they shall run out from their houses
and from their offices, all places of work,
and from the schools and training colleges,
from universities, from bars and taverns
into the streets, and yea, even there
shall be those who have beheld these things
upon their mobile telephone displays.
And there shall be great commotion and striving
for cars and taxis, all manner of transport,
public and private, to carry them out
to the air and heliports, so that the roads
are jammed, and there is much wailing and rage.
And those that reach the exit ports, they find

most tickets for Armageddon have been pre-sold,
and the few remaining priced beyond the means
of all but those of wealth and influence.
And of them that fly, even the most favoured,
many perish in the air collisions
resulting from the data overload
upon the systems for traffic control.
And many and congested are the flights
and the noises of their engines, and the crashing,
and the dark smoke of the burning,
that the sky is darkened with them,
so that some say: "Judgment is upon us here."
And of the number that fly those that reach
the landing places in sight of Armageddon
are but a tenth part, and of them again
that are landed safely are but a fifth part
(for the landing strips and fields are burning
and some cratered from the bombing,
so that planes are damaged or even wrecked
by reason of these fires and craters).
So of all that fly out those safely landed
at Armageddon are but a fiftieth part.
Yet even these number in their many thousands;
and they enter upon a scene of wonder,
the dead and mutilated being made whole
and rising, and more wonders to behold:
the tanks and other armoured vehicles,
the helicopter gun-ships, the missile launchers,
all manner of smart machines,
even those wrecked and burning,
are, as the dead, made whole and restored
unto their former state, as if the battle had not been.
And the nations, the people thereof
who have come from the four corners of the earth,
shall see all this military hardware rising
and taken up into the new Jerusalem,
and quiring angels round them singing
in praise of God.
                          And a great voice
out of heaven, saying: "Behold,
the tabernacle of God is with his people,
and God himself shall be with them and be their God."

And he that sitteth on the throne speaketh:
"Nations of the earth, ye who have come here,
my wrath is kindled against you,
for ye have not done the thing that is right,
as these my servants have. For these
have put themselves in danger for my sake,
as ye have not. For these have exposed
their flesh and metal to the chances of war and life,
as ye have not. Therefore ye shall not enter
the holy city, the new Jerusalem.
I have set aside another place for you,
a place for you as ye have lived,
the virtual Jerusalem.
Return ye now to your houses,
and to your offices, all places of work,
and to the schools and training colleges,
your universities, your bars and taverns,
there to look upon your viewing screens,
and into the streets, and yea, even there
to see upon your mobile telephone displays
the only Jerusalem of which you are worthy,
that ye shall have but shall not enter,
the after life as you have lived, virtually,
for evermore."

Beaureceuil

A long walk after the long lunch,
we in our party clothes. Meg found
it best to strip to petticoat,
unprepared for the unknown ground —
streams and boulders, the slipping crunch
of gravel, steep thorn woods, earth roads.
Bruno leading first, then Pierre,
round and up and down, and twice
at least it seemed we were returning.
Then out another stage to where
we saw and touched the Roman dam,
sighted the tower of Marius, learning
local facts, and crossed the race
that feeds those fountains down in Aix.
Uncanny silence of the flow
surging through its concrete box.
Tiredness beginning now,
mouth dry, hands blood pricked by thorn.
So through another wood, across
a hillside fire-scarred, a road
that curls and rises over there;
and next I know that's where I stand,
alone and looking back through air
in which my body walked. The land
beneath and far, that thin tree here,
the hillside fire-scarred, the white
and slanting grey Mont Sainte Victoire
in solemn distance, all are bright
embedded in a gleaming space,
the vacancy around these things,
a solid and transparent case
as dense and brilliant as these things.
So each contained in each, and all
in all; a unity perceived
by eye that breaks the common spell,
confirms the words that we've received
from those who claim to have seen God,
and which are meaningless until
the word's made flesh, the eye is fed
with vision and the mind is still.

A Cruel Winter

They execute the law that's everywhere,
these birds that come to take our seeds and crumbs.
They don't deserve this food; they haven't earned it.
They claim no right, no customary share.
They swoop and flutter down and take what comes.
They hop and stop and peck it, jab it, grab it.

These are the beasts of air who visit us,
exhibiting their natural neglect
of all proprieties to do with food,
and, leaving earth and us, leave us with this:
that we who are heavy with what we expect
have not the burden of their gratitude.

Spider

The spider has a right to live,
  As those sucked in her maw.
I squash the squalid little beast
  Between my shoe and floor.

Her right to live was issued with
  A free licence to kill.
Mine came hedged with doubts and fears
  And a questionnaire to fill:

Can I be justified to murder
  That which offends my sight?
Does my right imply a right
  To take another's right?

Right? What right? From whom? To whom?
  It sounds like politics.
This can't have anything to do
  With spiders, ants and ticks.

The spider dies beneath my foot
  Or is swirled down the drain.
The trees outside break into bud,
  Sap rising, thirst for rain.

The slimy slug insinuates
  Under the workshop door.
A heavy, hanging, smothering cloud
  Threatens, but cannot pour.

Discrete appearances provide
  The analytic view;
The world breaks down to acts and things,
  To me and it and you.

Oh, spider, I regret your death;
  Of you I am not free.
Your eight legs crawl about my soul
  Till something squashes me.

Eight for Dinner

As we are eight for dinner, they sit me
at the table's foot. Well, you know the form:
MF MF MF MF. I find
our hostess on my right and — with alarm —
on my left the bobbed blonde bore with no mind.
She bores straight in with bold inanity

and fixes me with her screwdriver stare.
Over the soup she starts: "Your ethnic roots"
(My what?) "must give you such a different view."
"Well…" "That's what I find differentiates."
"But I'm American." "Oh yes. Oh true.
But ethnically, I mean, you're Magyar."

"Now look. I was born in the USA,
was raised and educated there. My language
is English. I speak no Hungarian.
I do not carry any ethnic baggage.
And my father was not a full-grown man
but just a child when he crossed the sea.
Delicious soup. No thanks. I won't take more."
She smiles. It must mean now she knows the score.

Scene change. Next night. Rainswept road.
Car on move. Headlamps. Working wipers. Classic FM.
Hungarian Rhapsody Number 2
By Franz Liszt
                    list   *Oh list!*
If thou didst ever thy dear father love —
Oh black bright joy pain churning deep. I'm home!
Oh my father. Where is my love for you?

My Un-named Horror

This now before me is my un-named horror,
My curse, my penalty, my shadow beast,
My very own in a distorting mirror,
By me created or by me released,
Desire undesired, my truth, my terror.

Inverse, perverse. My anti-world. Is this
That self-same image Zoroaster met
Walking in the garden? The fateful hiss
Our parents heard in Paradise? A debt
To be called in, to pay for what I took
And bring a final balance to my book.

Hide and Seek

The game we play is hide and seek.
But you, my love, can't hide from me.
Wherever you may choose to flee,
Whatever new disguise you take,
    No need to search for you;
    You're always in full view.

Behind your hand, behind your face,
Crouching in your inner space,
Making love to lust and worry,
You're in my ancient territory.
   No need to seek you out;
   I know what you're about.

In fairness, then, I'll clue you in
The way that I am to be found.
    Like you
I'm hidden where I may be seen
And may be heard when there's no sound.

Between the light and the dark,
Between the glove and the hand,
Between the dog and its bark,
Between the sea and the sand.

Seek me in these hiding places;
Where I wait for your embraces.

Between the snail and its slime,
Between the stick and the drum,
Between the words of this rhyme,
Between what's gone and to come.

So don't be anxious, don't be clever;
I'm here, my love, for you forever.

Encounter

If you encounter me again
   how will you know it's me?
Look, now, this scene you recognize:
   the stream, the willow tree,

the old dilapidated barn,
   the ancient threshing floor —
you have no doubt; you know this place;
   you have been here before.

But I have been here all this time.
   I don't remember you.
Oh — could it be my memory
   is false and yours is true?

So tell me how you memorize.
   What is it you retain?
An image? But, my friend, that's just
   a phantom of the brain.

You say the image corresponds
   with what you see here now.
Of course it does, for corresponding
   images allow

your dear deceptive certainties
   to stiffen in the brain.
You, I, this place — we've never met
   nor ever will again.

Above Cwm Clyd

Below the Twmpa where some horses graze
I find by the fence Meg waiting for me.
I can't keep up with her, not now. These days
we walk apart-together. And then I see
close by, in innocence and helplessness,
the awkward grace of a long-legged foal,
so near its birth, and in life's wilderness
so near our neighbour Death. Eyes on patrol,
the group canters away into the mist.
Surprising how the foal with ease keeps up.
Those long legs of course — provided for just
this life-protective purpose, just as I stop,
on this walk struggling downward with these
my long-serving worn-out out-dated knees.

Infinity

I can't conceive infinity of space,
or space's end followed by nothingness.
Not quite true. What I can't is visualize.
My thinking is in thrall to my two eyes.
What is unseen and may in fact not be,
or be in otherness that eyes can't see,
incites the mind to recreate what's missed
in forms on which the questing eyes insist:

The Pantocrator staring from his dome,
angelic hosts, or dumb bull-headed might.
And seeing is believing. The old saw.
No miracles. The everyday at home.
The goddess on her round pausing in flight
to beckon one, who starts, wide-eyed with awe.

The Navigator

How does the navigator find his way
across the featureless and shifting seas?
He applies his skill to finding where he is;
the way to go then follows naturally.
Observe the paradox and subtlety:
he uses daylight only as it dies
or just before it brightens out the skies.
The twilight gloom shows what he needs to see:

Our earth and heaven in a balanced view —
those points of light the furthest from his sight
and the sea's far edge seen at the edge of night.
He reads degrees of arc between these two
that constant move, and marks the very instant,
and finds his place from what is dim and distant.

The Luohan

A moulded, glazed, ceramic man,
the inert image of a monk,
showed me, a soft, warm, breathing man,
how far from consciousness I'd sunk.

A zoo of images, this room.
there's clay, stone, patinated bronze,
and wizened wood in polychrome;
bought, stolen, smuggled — famous finds

separated from their sites
and divorced from their purposes,
displayed here under museum lights
to edify the populace.

The Chinaman there facing me —
tri-coloured, glistening smooth — shows no
response to his captivity,
doesn't fret on his plinth or grow

surly and spit at visitors.
He cannot suffer, cannot die.
He cannot sleep. Although of course
he can be smashed up — as can we.

He's just an image of a man
long dead, or one who had no life,
but was imagined. Yet that man,
unreal or dead, knows more of life

and death, and death in life, and life
in death, than I have ever known.
And he asks me to wake to life,
like him to be, by means unknown.

Sitting we watch the living dead
who wander through his room, their eyes
dim with respect, hushed comments made,
and not much seen. My world, not his.

The Shadow

On the naked branch I was the sparrow
Dipping and swaying in the ice cold wind.
And at the kitchen window stood the shadow
 Peering through the pane.
 And what is life but sorrow?
 There is no end to wind,
 The hollow howl and bite,
 And I must face the wind
 To keep my feathers tight.
 And now the freezing rain.

And then I was the brave, wave-battered boat
Beating to windward, dancing in the spray.
And on the shore the shadow, wrapped in coat
 And scarf, with salt on lips.
 And life is death afloat.
 The great supporting sea,
 My very element,
 Tries to capsize me.
 I head up to confront
 The murderer of ships.

Today I am the de-faced, weather-worn
Colossus, split by tremor to the waist.
I have been known to sing and sigh at dawn,
 They say to greet my mother.
 So life calls out from stone.
 The shadow dreams the taste
 Of centuries like mine,
 Glances to the east
 Where he would see a sign.
 No age is like another.

Tomorrow then what shall I be? What thing
Will catch the shadow's eye? What momentary
Imagined correspondence will I bring
    To tempt him to distraction?
    I could be anything.
    My form and substance vary,
    Though constant to my theme,
    Immortal, never weary,
    The god of waking dream,
    The monarch of inaction.

Universe

If the universe is infinite,
then I am its centre,
and so are you.
And this holds true
wherever we go.
We cannot escape
our significance.

The Annunciation

In Rogier van der Weyden's Annunciation
The Holy Ghost enters the Virgin's chamber
As a dove gliding on a beam of light —
Pre-figuring the coming act
Through this illuminating penetration
That leaves the purity of glass intact.

But what of the furnace and the crucible?
The sweat and stress of fire-darkened men,
The makers of the innocence of glass from sand?
And when the mighty maker, lord of life,
The maker of his mother's flesh from dust,
Is re-made in his mother's flesh – again:
What of the sweat and stress? The blood? The cord
    that's cut?
It's only the conception that's immaculate.

Reading

What a curious thing reading is.
A carriageful of people, different sorts,
and most are staring, staring silently
at different sized rectangular pieces
of paper — like dumb beasts who think (if that's
the word) there might be something there they see

that could be eaten if it moved. And then
their bodies as they stare are covered by
or draped in various cloths, just leaving free
their heads and both front paws. They sit upon
their rumps. From time to time one will put by
its paper, rise and walk erect. I see

their transparent reflections in the dark
racing past houses, street lamps, trees. They seem
lost in some lunar process, unaware
of the world shining through them, as they make
their good time effortlessly towards home —
to forest, mountain, field — or abattoir.

Nunquam Reditura

High on the sun-bright wall
of the barn on Bredon Hill
the shadow of the gnomon
lies stark and dark and still.

So say the eyes, who take
impression and no more,
and leave the timeless moment
no memory in store.

It is the mind that knows,
recording what is seen.
It knows the shadow moves,
remembers what has been.

And if the day is dimmed
with cloud and rising mist,
and dial speaks to eyes,
says time does not exist,

another shadow falls
across the inward gaze,
and this the mind can read
even on darkest days.

And when the burning sun
drops down from its high climb,
and the greater shadow soon
obliterates the time,

the mind remembers how
the telling-time restarts,
for the dial is contained
within its moving parts.

The going train's the earth,
the driving weight's the sun;
both show and make the time
till all our time is done.

Twilight

It's fun: really, we bought it for the view,
She said, turning back from the dimming light.
Time's running out for us. What can we do?

A pause. Already we could scent the dew,
Anticipate the owls in their flight.
It's fun: really, we bought it for the view.

We'll plant a hedge of beech or, John thinks, yew,
To hide that horrid thing. It is a blight.
Time's running out for us. What can we do?

The orchard's overgrown. Much, much to do.
Now pupils dilate with the loss of light.
It's fun: really, we bought it for the view.

Inside, the reek of damp. *Oh, that will go.*
Her wings, and mine, are folded out of sight,
Time's running out for us. What can we do?

And angels sleep worldwide. The devil's due.
His drowsy swarms are driving through the night.
It's fun: really, we bought it for the view.
Time's running out for us. What can we do?

Life v. Death

I'm absolutely terrified of Life.
It's everywhere; it's taking over. Death
is losing out; it can't last. Beneath
this ground corpses are rotting to breed more Life.
The graves are hotbeds of it. Death makes Life.
We kill to eat, but our excrement
is stinking with resurgence. Food that's spent
starts out again with viscid putrid Life.

Where will it end? It won't. It can't. Inert,
Death has no future, and Life, having no aim
other than self increase, suffers no hurt.
Oh Death, where is thy sting? Undone by slime;
the uni-cellular plan set to win:
divide and conquer at the origin.

Love?

Love? It's all just atoms and the void.
Does he believe that? No, it comforts him
to say so — a sort of self-protective whim —
as some might spin a doctrine out of Freud
to reduce all fond emotion to the beast.
But he is limitless in ridicule:
it's back to basics, to the molecule,
reducing what is greatest to the least.

The pose, dispassionate analysis,
the escape-hatch of the scientific mind,
as with a weary, condescending air
he patiently points out the obvious —
the pretence of the bully to be kind,
whose ending and beginning is despair.

Storm at Sea

Losing my way one heaving, stormy night,
I blundered onto the bridge — where perhaps
I was not meant to be — and there took fright:
the wheel untended, no one there! *Who keeps
the watch?* my former naval voice called out,
unheard by winking, clicking instruments.
Green water shuddered ship and me. I sensed
my body then, the self-adjusting beat
of pumping blood, the intake and exhaust
of breath — which all was being done for me
as it has for decades, faultlessly.
So where and when do I come in? The tossed
and trembling ship! and who is meant to man it?
And who or what has just composed this sonnet?

April Morning

My morning visit where she lies
down in the passage on her bed,
she does not know what I know: dread —
before the morning's gone she dies.

I wrap her in the yellow towel
and take her up. Again how warm
that frail, dependent body; from harm
I should defend her, keep her well.

Her trust is absolute like faith:
I am protector and provider,
connected with that pulse inside her;
and I am lord of life and death.

One paw, in spasm or intent,
pokes out as if to point the way.
I bring her to the grass and try
to stand her upright, thin legs bent.

I hold her there and then let go;
at once she collapses on her bum
and waits, whatever is to come.
Ambitionless it's ever so.

Here now, and no thought for tomorrow;
and you don't flesh your bones in thought,
remember youth and rabbits caught
and wonder at time's waste in sorrow.

My little leaping lovely friend,
eager, barking, quick and darting,
ever bright, alert and marking
every gesture, mood, command.

I'd call your name; you'd skid, spin round.
And once in quiet space I spoke
with inner voice commands you took
in purity, no need of sound,

we two in silence tuned to one.
Now shading close to twenty years,
no use of eyes, no use of ears;
silence enforced, not silence won.

All powers failing round the core
where beats that heart, the vet told me,
is strangely strong, too strong, you see,
for the wasted frame it's working for.

The vet is good, no messing about,
assuring me as I stroke your head
you'll feel no pain, you'll soon be dead.
The needle goes in, and you go out,

transformed into a memory.
We undo your collar, take your towel;
at home there's lead, brush, comb and bowl.
What shall we with this legacy?

No more Blackie seen or heard:
down in the passage on her bed
in miniature a pyramid,
her last: a firm, moist, yellow turd.

A message to the world of things
beyond the source of age and youth,
the suave brutality of truth
that crushes my imaginings.

The Wind

for Anne, who asked for an
explanation of the wind in verse

A restless spirit is the wind,
veering and backing as it blows,
seeking what it cannot find,
a haven for its own repose.

Inherent failure in this quest,
a lesson in futility;
for if it found its place of rest,
what joy? It will have ceased to be.

But that is what all nature wants,
the most pathetic fallacy:
it is the universal dance
of death, the term is entropy.

The clock runs down, the kettle cools,
the batteries go dead — unless,
attentive to a need, what rules
these things restores their liveliness.

Re-wind, re-heat, re-charge — but who,
or what, re-winds the wind? what guide
directs it rather to renew
than lapse to gradual suicide?

Expansion makes the hot air rise;
contraction makes the cool air fall;
the wind moves both to equalise.
So when that's done there's rest for all.

Not quite. There's more to this equation
than air and heat alone: the earth
itself, its axial rotation,
the eccentric tilt, and round its girth

the geographic complication
of mountains, deserts and the seas
that swing in tidal variation —
all these irregularities

obstruct the wind's entropic course.
But what obstructs the earth's decline?
and what about the universe?
Here some propose a thing divine —

unique causation, first and final,
the unmoved mover, *causa sui*,
Aristotelian or Aquinal,
ruling heaven, earth and sea.

But this is now beyond my scope.
I've answered you as best I can.
What's left for me is now to hope
that what I've writ may please you, Anne.

To the Reader

Reader, as you exist in time,
Unriddle me this simple rhyme:
I'm older than my older brother;
I'm even older than my mother.
My father still out-ages me,
But as I live and gather time
I'll out-age him. How can this be?

As I said, it's simple. Yes,
You've worked it out. No need to guess.
They're dead, stone dead — petrified
In time that stopped dead when they died.
And should I see my mother now
In everlasting loveliness,
I'd comfort her and tell her how

Her infant son survived her ghastly
Going, nourished by her ghostly
Love. I'd tell my brother mentor
He is my mentor still. And sent or
Summoned to my father, we'd see
Our closeness now, though mistily,
That never as we lived could be.

A Song for My Family

My father and my brother,
My step and my real mother
Are gone. Yet here alone,
Unreached by touch or phone,
The residues of three
Breathe in and out through me;
I'm host to my dead family.

My father finished well:
In his garden he fell
Heartstruck near the stone wall
He built, and hid from all
For hours till they found him,
The plants he loved around him.
Too late for me who never found him.

My brother never finished:
Without fair cause was banished
From me, from wife, from sons,
To where the dark stream runs,
No more allowed to live,
Heartstruck, no more to give.
I am his representative.

The step, really my aunt,
Would scold and hit and rant
Or snarl and disapprove.
Negation was her love,
Which she did not forsake,
Drowned herself in the lake.
And I must breathe now for her sake.

Then where is mother found?
Deep within the wound.
Run down when I was three,
Flesh buried in the ground,
Love buried inside me,
And with it memory.
So gone, yet still possessed by me.

Not dead, buried alive
To make her love survive.
But love entombed is lost
I know to my steep cost.
A treasure's of no worth
When buried in the earth.
My mother, I must give you birth.

The Season Turns

The season turns. We will be flying south,
the left land loud with our cries of passage,
the sunlight scattered by our wings — a message
encrypted on the sky for those on earth.
And soon the tangled towns recede, give way
to uplands stretching to the cliff-hung shore,
where soundless is the sea's incoming roar
as our shadows slip the breakers of the bay.

Absence is the condition of our presence.
Neither citizen nor alien,
we move between the lightness and the dark,
streaming out on the great magnetic arc,
in isolated height, allied to none,
our flight the unfurled flag of our allegiance.

Out of Greece

Somatianá

A snake has left its skin behind
    hanging from a nail.
We leave it there for we've been told
    good fortune will not fail
as long as it remains. A venomous
    visitor has come
and gone, discarding this thin sheath
    that's now a magic charm,
like other desiccated scraps
    of strange anatomies
and bones and bits of martyred saints
    preserved in reliquaries.
But we will not preserve, protect
    or cherish what we're given.
We'll let it rot and drop, but keep
    the lesson:
to slough off what's ephemeral
    and move on.

Belonging

*The poet as a stranger contemplates
the unity of all things*

Walking through our village
where we do not belong —
as Charmian said at lunch —
and never can belong —

sunset stretches wide
the Messinian Gulf;
orange flares pink and fades
withdrawing to itself.

We pick our way along
the stone strewn path back home.
Our darkening mountain rears
ridge hooded with its gleam

from earth's pale prisoner,
the stone-cold light of night,
while round my wrist I feel
another satellite,

a disc of jewelled steel
that's keeping time for me,
as moons and planets do,
turning quietly.

It's swinging with my arm
on my sinister side
scribing pendular arcs,
measuring my stride —

unconscious as my blood
in vein and artery
is shadowing the stars
in liquid circuitry —

where corpuscles obey
the universal beat —
and steps in twilight down
this Greek and crooked street.

A stone is kicked and tumbles —
through interstellar tracks —
ellipses of the moons —
Parsecs! Parallax!

Taygetos

I.

The pair of buzzards climb on rising air,
tilt from the sun, drift up along the gorge,
and over the top crag are gone, to where
they hold their raptor mysteries, and merge
in mind with other flying carnivores
lodging on similar inhuman heights —
the deathless gods who regulate the world
and eye us transients scattered round the floors
of their delightful imperial estates.
At times they favour us, when we are old
or very young, with glimpses of their forms;
at other times disguised as mortal beasts
they infiltrate our ordinary days.
But we, obsessed with creeds and false alarms,
no longer offer sacrificial feasts.
Firmly believing gods and myths are lies,
we're unprepared for visits from the skies.

II.

A year ago I wrote a poem here,
its theme suggested by a pair of birds
of prey, and, ever anxious that my words
be accurate, that what I make appear
in verse be true to what I've seen, I sought
in a book of birds their right identity.
Alas — it offered choice, not certainty:
either a type of large buzzard, I thought,
or, not unlikely, the short-toed eagle. Well,
alert to that temptation to dress up
my poem with borrowed grandeur, in the hope
of Miltonic favours from the world, and all
my gathered modesty before creation
inhibiting excess, I settled for
the buzzard. Then today by chance I saw
along the mountain's seaward elevation
one of those impressive birds again. I
was higher, it was closer, on my level,
allowing me to see clearly the several
pointers needed to identify

and discriminate — round owl-like head,
long tail, long straightish wings, black primaries,
white underneath, powerful flight, right size,
in every detail true to what I'd read: —
the eagle — winging through my afternoon,
passing close, strange as the distant moon;
and I, alive with wonder at this bird,
forgot the poet who dithers at a word.

Lunch in Kardamyli

The caïque there rests at anchor, rocking
to the undulant chaos of the wavelets
and the low swells incoming, intersecting.
A solitary boat, the bright sea sparkling;
this view is all we harbour in perception.

And here the voices at that other table —
decisive, questioning, deferential —
flowing from Greek through English — courteous talk —
and back from German through the same, now Greek
that English was — so suave, so multi-lingual.

How overwhelmingly massive the sea!
How secretive the dark and bitter depths!
We hear the touch of glass to glass to glass,
a phrase re-echoing from voice to voice,
beneath this shade of canopied bamboo,
so amiable the heat of day to view.
How overwhelmingly massive the sea!
How secretive the dark and bitter depths!

The Moon and Mars in Mani

Later each night appears the hump-backed Moon,
waxing, and rising in retard, so that bright Mars
is closing up behind, and soon
will overtake — as seen, that is, in flat
projection on the non-existent dome
we apprehend as our celestial map —
while here each day the two Albans resume
at early light their patient work to prop
our neighbour's house. Up towards the sagging roof
stones rise. One sets the spirit level to lie
along the vertical to test for truth,
applying the self-same law of gravity
that holds in their orbits the Moon and Mars
and regulates infinities of stars.

Principles of Human Knowledge at Ayios Nikolaos

The surging rollers, remnants of a storm
remote in time and place, are crashing now
on this sea-wall, and I'm observing how
the tethered boats, secure enough from harm,
as if in mute and modest celebration
pitch and roll each in its unique mode
of cyclical responsive movement, owed
to varying displacement and position;
and this tripod table on the rough stone floor,
how it securely upholds what we drink:
we know in practice, whatever we may think,
what Euclid knew: three legs are better than four.

The Berkeley book lies face down on this table,
his image on the cover out of sight,
and out of mind, as he would say, his flight
of intellectual fancy made to enable
a logical proof of the necessary
existence of God. But I am wary
of the Bishop's philosophical intent,
as his belief precedes his argument —
which goes something like this: what we perceive
is all we know, with no cause to believe
that outside this there is reality.
To be in mind is what it is to be.
If something then continues to exist
when it no longer is perceived by me —
his face, let's say — another mind must be.
So for the world entire to persist
in being there needs a universal mind.
We see where this is leading. Not hard to find.

The mind of God retains the Bishop's face,
and in that nowhere all things have their place:
the storm, the time, the distance and the boats,
the book rejected and the thoughts it brings,
how I observe this dance of lifeless things,
the lively tugging at their lines and floats
the while their owners idle on the quay
reading the future from the day that's gone,
the slab that will display no catch at dawn,
the cold, dry marble and the surging sea.

On Blake on a Beach

While lounging on a windy beach
of Magna Graecia, the sands
philosophers have used to teach
are sifting through my sun-browned hands.

And memory brings mystic lines
from one who scorned the rational,
for whom all things were holy signs
and pure the inexplicable.

"Mock on," he said to men of mind,
"Mock on, mock on, 'tis all in vain.
You throw the sand against the wind,
and the wind blows it back again."

"The atoms of Democritus
and Newton's particles of light"
are sands he said are blinding us
who think the mind a form of sight.

The vanity of mental search
for what the smallest thing might be —
oh, William, from your lonely perch
could you not see the poetry?

If in a volume we collect
your poems, as a metaphor,
to be the world, and then inspect
the composition of that store,

we find we can divide the book
into the separate poems there,
and then, as we more closely look,
divisions subsequent appear:

into stanzas first, then to lines,
to phrases, then to single words,
and then to those enscripted signs —
the letters that make up the words.

And here we make discovery:
than letters there is nothing less.
We've reached the end linguistically;
division here is meaningless.

So now we know the smallest thing
has not to do with size or state:
it's where our means of questioning
dissolve — that is the ultimate.

Using the metaphor as guide,
the subtlety of mind can see
what visionaries seek to hide
and find a limit to what can be.

It's rather, William, you who mock,
with vision darken and impose.
Humility is theirs who look
where nature offers to disclose.

Orpheus

I.

The Gods have all been summoned to attend
Olympian Zeus. Once they've gathered round
he speaks: "What's happened now? Where are the prayers
of humankind? Have they forgot us? The fires
of sacrifice even now we see below,
pillars of smoke coiling in upward flow.
But to what purpose? No words ascend,
no praise, no promises, no pleas to mend
or overcome. The scent of roasting meat
is rancid without prayer to make it sweet.
Hermes, my youngest son, it's you who taught
them how to offer sacrifice — the art
of sacred butchery, the ritual
of act and spoken word. Indeed, all
their eloquence of speech is in your care.
So tell us: why have they abandoned prayer?"

The artful messenger replies:
"Although I care, I can't control.
They pray, but each itself denies,
for human speech has lost its soul,
and soul-less words can't reach the skies."

"Alone among the earthly creatures,
formed like us, with god-like features,
we offered them the power of words
so they could speak with us their lords,
the world of sense to represent,
necessity and accident,
and thoughts escaping mortal reach
yet be reflected in their speech.
The fault in this perhaps is ours:
to expect, as they resemble us
in superficial form, that thus
they'd manage without loss of ease
the subtle sightless energies
of mind. Yet as experiment
it verified our confident

appraisal — for a time — until,
that is, a gift of mortal will,
entangled the original
with new seductive benefit.
This device, called the Alphabet,
converts the words that live as sound
to aggregates of marks we find
now scribed on stones and daubed on skins.
Forgetful of the origins,
released from need to memorize,
their words meant not for ears, but eyes,
they've put aside formality
of sonic pulse and harmony.
With untuned words designed for sight
their speaking mimics how they write,
where form is naught, and matter's all,
and thus unfit for ritual.
However they may solemnise
or shake the air with desperate cries,
what gifts they bring or fasts endure,
their thought be whole and purpose pure,
no prayer from them can touch our sense.
As born, it dies. No resonance
persists.

      This oblate sphere, its turn
through orbiting and axial spin,
mediating among the stars,
partaking of effect and cause,
where each consistent, minute grain
presents an image of the main,
is itself an image, for these are but
the apparitions that reflect,
in play of light and dark, the core
that's neither light nor dark, but more
than both. When smallest elements
combine in mass that human sense
perceives, it's as it were a gesture
translating energy to vesture,
disclosing and concealing form.
Be it star or stone, God or worm,
the cosmic pulse and harmony
is what it is we share to be.
But mortal speech is alien

to this: with chisel, knife and pen
they've made a specious permanence
that beguiles the mind and tempts
them to assign to what they see
a sensible reality.
The mighty Lexicon, denied
its purpose, to illusion tied,
usurps the wordless world it's meant
symbolically to represent;
and they for whom the world is named,
convinced it's known, possessed and tamed,
mistake the word for the thing,
their knowing naught but labelling;
and so the act, and so the thought;
their understanding has been caught,
bewitched by our divine gift.
What we prepared so they could lift
the limits of mortality
provokes a fall: — from unity
into division, from innocence
to cultivated ignorance,
from sacred commerce with their lords
to futile fantasies of words."

"Then how is speech to be redeemed?" asks Zeus.
"However it be maimed by perverse use,
we'll not withdraw what we have freely given.
The rule is nature, if the source be Heaven.
We will not interfere; we must contrive
an influence for which, though it derive
from us, the instrument be incarnate;
so they be free to accept or deny,
and we respect their one immortal part:
the conscious will. In this we rectify
our fault. The presentation of a gift
is in disguise a subtle form of thrift:
they who receive, deceived, cannot possess
what is, remains, the patron's own largesse;
and are in debt for what they do not have,
by what they do have made the poorer. Love
does not adhere to such, nor proper fear.
Yet now, divorced from what they would hold dear
and bound to artifice, bound to resist

what defies their need to define and list,
to separate, enumerate, to break
in parts, disintegrate and so unmake
into a prosperous illusion, they —
these muted separates from heaven — may,
in want of wakeful will, despite the chance,
drowse out epiphany — deliverance
not sought, not prized, not found, the avatar
applauded with neglect, a sinking star
to rise again and re-rise on his arc,
immortal so and ever in the dark,
and ever dark returning — even this
to partake of the pulse of wilderness.
Redemption's not for now, nor forever,
not for the simple, nor the clever,
nor the warlike, nor the peaceable:
only a strangely clear, recurrent call
for some or few or one — or none at all —
who in their star-lit dark have will to be.
Where one thing ends and another begins
they'll see the entrails of infinity;
when one side loses and another wins
they'll hear the heartbeat of eternity."

II.

Olympic hope informs the chosen means,
the genesis of action by the Gods,
foreknowledge not of certainty, but odds.

So Orpheus:
                    they smuggled him
to earth inside a Muse's womb,
she who with a Thracian king
had shared a bed, conveniently
through casual love establishing
a plausible paternity.
The royal infant soon received
a visitation from the God
his father, as by most believed,
Apollo, Lord of Light, the bed
he now approached already heaped

and strewn about with princely gifts —
from friends and allies, and those who hoped
to be so — fashioned by the crafts
of smith and armourer in bronze
and gold with orient gems inset,
the warlike splendour fit for sons
of kings. Through these on naked foot
soft stepping, Apollo placed beside
the sleeping head of Orpheus
an instrument a God had made,
primitive and ingenious,
from a tortoise-shell and sliced cow-gut: —
the lyre of seven strings.
                                    His aunts,
the Muses, later would instruct
the child in the resonance
of intervals, the tetrachords,
the tones and semi-tones, the dance
inducing patterns that, his words
accompanying, would resound
within the singer and without —
instant knowing that knows no doubt,
unknown to be as it dies out
when he dies out, till it's re-found
through rapturous intelligence
after the Muse's long retreat
full many generations hence.
Apollo also will retreat,
for, though Gods' lives are limitless,
their power is on condition held,
and when their sacred wilderness
is confiscate they are expelled.
One alone, the great God Pan,
has been reported dead; but this,
the hearsay of one sailor man,
is belied by the persistent trace,
his goatish presence that's still felt
in certain secluded caves and woods.
Exiled Apollo it's said has dwelt
and worked through various interludes,
mostly as herdsman, moving on
from each before he's recognised.
Once, singing near a northern town,

he was spied on by a local priest.
"This man's a pagan God disguised,"
declared the learned cleric. Seized,
Phoebus was sent for trial. On
the rack he readily confessed
he was the Lord Apollo. "Can
I be allowed," he begged, "at least
to sing and play upon the lyre
one final song before I die?"
Granted this humble, last desire,
his words and notes so magically
combined that men were brought to tears,
and women swooned and at his death
fell sick, so that the priest had fears
Phoebus had laid with his last breath
a curse on women, who are weak.
He told the men to drag the fiend
back from the grave and drive a stake
right through his heart, that thus an end
to him and his foul curse be made.
The men went with this purpose, but
the priest's words could not be obeyed.
Empty was the opened grave.
                                        Yet,
the vagrant Gods themselves when prime
were not renowned for merciful
or just considering of crime
or innocent occasional
affronts to their supremacy,
and cruel and unusual
the punishments they could decree.
Theirs the finest apprehension;
thus quick to sense and suffer slight,
and quick to anger, as the intention
was acted fact, such their might.
When Athena played the double flute
she had just fashioned from a pair
of bones, she carefully took note
of Aphrodite hiding her
smiling, silent mockery
behind a delicate, lifted hand.
Withdrawing from all company,
and taking to the sloping sand

beside a glassy stream, she played
to her self-reflected audience,
and saw at once her shame displayed:
the red, swollen cheeks! A howl, a wince.
In fury she threw down the flute
and laid a curse on it and any
who dared to take it up.
                        A brute
of nature — why he out of the many?
Here is no certainty, just odds,
the law of accident, always
in force — this Satyr of the woods,
doomed Marsyas, sees, takes and plays.
And did the cursed instrument
retain as well the Memory
of her? With no accomplishment
Marsyas is beguiled to vainglory,
so gorgeous, so melodious,
so various the music he
can inattentively produce,
his fingers, breath as if they be
as instrumental as the flute,
playing and played all three as one.
Air, energy and bone transmute:
what is becomes else and is gone.
The going and becoming make
of gain a loss, of loss a gain;
the time and tone together take
away what is yet does remain.
All those in hearing distance now
begin to approach and gather round
to see what God has come below
to entertain them with a sound
so piercing strange, though as returning.
A double marvel: what they hear,
now what they see. Look, without learning
or any need to persevere
it's Marsyas playing like a God.
And some declare even Apollo
could do no better.
                     A hint of dread
as Marsyas senses what may follow.
No sooner sensed than seen. Among

the crowd the smiling God appears,
cradling his lyre, ready strung
and tuned. To Marsyas as he nears
a hand offered in recognition.
"They seem to claim that you may be
as estimable a musician
as on the lyre I'm known to be.
So let us have a competition
in open here by this pine tree.
To the Muses I have made submission
that they should judge, and they agree.
And I suggest just one condition:
no prize, instead the victor chooses
a penalty that he who loses
must pay at once and on this spot.
So all that's liable is what he's got.
Now — if you win, it's lasting fame.
What say you, Marsyas, are you game?"
The Satyr thinks, he must refuse;
he cannot win, or if he should,
however won, he still will lose;
you can not, must not, test a God.
But can you, dare you, to his face
turn down an offer from a God?
That were to expose him to disgrace
in public here before a crowd.
To them he turns, give they a sign?
They're all intent, waiting on him;
only the whispers of the pine,
the swirl and bubble of the stream.
"My lord, how can I not accept
the honour your kind invitation
has just conferred on me? I'm trapped —
I mean, there is no other option,
is there?"
                    Apollo indicates
a place to sit beside the tree;
he sits the other side and waits,
the lyre resting on his knee.
The Muses on the bank appear;
(eight only out of nine, for one
is pregnant, and her time is near)
they nod, the contest to begin.

Say, Memory, who was it first
drew sound in concert each alone?
Was it the God or the man-beast?
The gut-strung shell or double-bone?

Trying his best behaviour,
no confidence in skill or luck,
the Satyr makes as to defer;
Apollo has already struck
the opening heraldic chord.
They say — those fortunate enough
to witness there and to have heard
the airborne beauty born of strife —
the chord contained and was prelude
to a persistent, simple tune,
to which in deferential mode
the Satyr answered struck with blown.
A variation followed, varied
again in dark renewal where
inversion of the first was buried,
returned in flute, recalled to lyre,
and soon the answers came before
the interrogation could complete,
questioning the questioner,
combining in creative heat.
The strike and pipe abolish time,
anticipation unified;
each knowing each, they both become
another music deified.
The witnesses' remembering:
a secret, other world revealed,
where every separate act and thing
is joined, all differences healed.

The music generates its rest
upon a vacancy of sound,
as if the playing was a quest
for what they now together find:
a silence vast and intimate.
The Muse whose face is never seen
speaks: "These two as one have met;
our judgement cannot come between."
"But we're not done," Apollo says

as he retunes his instrument,
"Come, do as I do, Marsyas:
sing and play accompaniment."
He strokes the strings and sings a hymn
praising the Olympian Gods.
The moment's glowing hope grows dim
as certainty replaces odds.
The chastening beauty of the song,
for which the vacancy was made,
enters every living thing,
including he who's to be flayed.

A second silence Marsyas breaks:
"My lord, you've won; my music's mute.
what penalty my lord now takes?
Take all I have, this precious flute."

"That whistling pipe is not for me;
I've proved its insufficiency.
What I shall take to mark my win
is your entire, living skin."
New sound succeeds, new vacancy:
a screaming Satyr, a silent crowd.
Inverted, hanging from the tree,
he's skinned like game brought down for food.
The carcase in the stream is heaved,
red swatches swirling to the sea.
A proclamation is perceived:
the skin nailed firmly to the tree.

What of the flute now twice discarded?
Where dropped it lies in Satyr's blood.
Exeunt omnes, scene recorded.
A younger God comes from the wood,
with vine leaves woven through his hair,
looks down, takes up the pair of pipes
and blows announcement to the air,
his fingers bloodied on the stops.

III.

Will the newborn know what's been prepared
through conscious will and accident

entwined? both honoured and both feared,
the source of all accomplishment?

The question's begged of what it is
to know. Fate, destiny seem true
only in retrospect; yet, as
the hour comes, one cries: "I knew!"

The Muses take their sister's son
and bathe him in those sacred springs
that rise upon Mount Helicon
and neighbouring Parnassos — things
and thoughts, sensations, acts — all claims
of difference — symbolically
dissolved in cool ablutive streams
cascading to the seamless sea,
where, disengaged from definition,
in disappearing become free.
Then ready for the first tuition,
each one a note, between each two
an interval, the Muses start
the dance of octaves, moving through
the scaled modalities where art
and nature meet. Orpheus prepared
by sight, he will remember when
with breaking voice and hint of beard,
and having learnt the words of men,
he finds his way back to this height
and takes position in the dance,
the apex note that binds the eight
and by them bound in resonance.
Throughout the figure moves the word
along the chords that intersect,
mutual energy transferred
between the heart and intellect.

From dawn through daylight to the dusk,
from dusk through darkness to the dawn,
the daughters of Memory guide
the youth and celebrate the task.
The seeds of sacrifice are sown,
the dance descends the mountainside.

Duality of written word and sound,

uncertainty of particle and wave —
Orpheus is the unity will save
what's born to die, what's lost so to be found.
How do we measure time? This globe that seems
so ponderous in our waking dreams,
on its imaginary axis turning
so clear in our deceived discerning,
in space its hardly visible rotation
has whirled a thousand miles in the duration
of Orpheus' climb down to the plain.
How many moments does an hour contain?
How long is a minute? how short? We fail,
seeking to measure time, for time's the scale,
a conceptual necessity
through which we organise reality,
but of whose nature it does not partake.

The bedrock of illusion: time is fake.
How can time exist when each of its parts
that makes the sum, each moment, as it starts
is at its end? The sum of such is naught.
Or if we try with systematic thought
precisely to locate each moment's end,
all our suppositions will contend
with what we ask: not now, for now it is;
not the next moment, for when is that? nor does
it cease in subsequence, for that's too late.
We're left to join with those who speculate
about eternal presence, so that now
and then together make a total now,
which, as we saw above, adds up to naught.
Yet all perceived events, however short,
have temporal duration.
                              How can that be?
Not be, but sensed — through death and memory.
Complete existence is as music played:
to give time to the next each note must die,
for of successive deaths is music made
and held suspended, live, in memory.

Is he remembered, Orpheus?
We've heard, and seen in written text,
how with his gifted lyre and voice

he charmed both this world and the next.

Duality of written word and sound,
uncertainty of particles and waves,
Orpheus is the unity that saves
what's born to die, what's lost so to be found.

What can be said and what cannot,
the Lexicon and Nature meet,
combine in ecstasy complete:
the re-discovered soul's begot.
All nature, raised in resonance,
quickens to the man-god's art,
as if of nature new all start
to celebrate in Orphic dance.
Birds, beasts, predators and game,
furred or feathered, wild and tame:
all follow. Fish leap and leave their place,
tails skipping on the water's face.
Tall trees strain at their roots, we're told,
and some break out from earth's firm hold.
Another poet did report
a stand of oaks — this one may doubt —
in Hellenistic time were found
positioned in the perfect round
they occupied when the dancing stopped.
Those huge stones seen erect, unpropped,
in ancient circles are, some say,
more wondrous relics of that day.
One creature, though, did not partake.
My rhyme foretells: the lowly snake,
who answers but the solo flute,
and still does if the player's astute.
This metonymic fellow was
the ever-lurking mechanism
pre-set for circumstance to close
the dance with sudden spasm
of human pain and loss. For two
in one is the man-god that's sent:
the one alone to rendezvous
with fate, and one with accident.
Down from Parnassos to the plain,
and now begins the next descent,

the first link of the causal chain
forged in the heat of ravishment.
Say, Memory, did he ask:
"Why she?" and did she ask: "Why me?"
and did he undermine the task
in singing for Eurydice?
Surely was she beguiled by
the focus focussing on her,
and surely she was envied by
those girls who whirled about the star,
and likely he was hated by
the boy who loved her, Aristaeus,
who pleads and begs, demands, insists,
grasps her in desperate embrace.
She squirms and beats with tiny fists,
demolishing his hope. He drops
his ineffectual arms. Thus free,
she turns and runs and, running, steps
where accident and death agree.
The venom that the fangs inject
is teleologically refined:
nor love nor pity can deflect
the aim for which it is designed.

How pain seems long, and life seems brief;
her very going is her grief.

The boy's already torn from bliss.
Rejection is the sharper hurt:
that's personal. This second loss:
no urge to groan and tear his shirt;
she's also lost to Orpheus.

Desire, love, possession are
the vertices between the sides
that meet in shape triangular
where they and nothing else abides.

The poet-prince, despite what some
suppose, did neither grieve nor mourn.
Once her remains were in the tomb
he counselled all: "Be not forlorn.
You've seen how I have charmed the world,
how creatures, things, however strong,

gave up their natures to my song.
So shall as well the underworld."

IV.

The mouth of Hades at Tenaron,
where Mount Taygetos trails its spine
into the sea, a cave half brine,
half rock, through which to pass a man
must swim, and slide, then crawl, before
the sunlit radiance sdims to dark,
the ceiling lifts, and he can walk
upon that sombre, inner shore.
Now vision is with sense, not sight;
the living man must have the skill
to use what Death can never kill,
which is the memory of light.
For know there are three worlds: the one
that is, the one that we perceive,
and the one we go to when we leave.
Here Orpheus is set upon
his inward journey. He apprehends
the tertiary mode of being;
he's learnt the secret mode of seeing;
he's polished and made clean the lens
of memory. What was appears
again in Death.
                      The guardians
of access to that vague expanse,
attentive as the music nears,
become compliant to his need:
the surly boatman poles him across
the mist-hung river; Cerberus,
the monster with three mouths to feed,
relaxes, wags his single tail
and trebly licks the poet's feet.
The lesser demons make retreat
along the murky, jagged trail
to Tartarus, hopping and prancing
to the harmony and vital beat,
the melodies so bittersweet,
compelling all, and all entrancing,

as on the gruesome halls advancing,
the Furies weep, with pity seized;
the tortures of the damned are eased;
spellbound is Hell by necromancing.
The moans and blubberings subside,
the prisoners recover speech;
to the poet as he passes each
expostulates and would confide
his history and ask for news,
for prayers to be sent below —
though hope is lost, you never know —
but as he passes through they lose
their moments dreamed within the dream.
Enchantment wanes, as when the wind
to litter and dry leaves may lend
false animation so they seem
as self-propelled, until the gust
abandons them. Such is the art
of Orpheus, the counterpart
of the active principle lost
in Death. Now, as the howls of Hell
re-echo and recede, those neither
damned nor blest appear, who linger
apart in fields of asphodel,
without cheer, prospect or intent,
their life in death as death in life
that was, avoidance of all strife,
and they alone indifferent
even to Orpheus. His song
concentrically diminishes
as it expands and finishes
unheeded, unremarked along
the unfeatured limits of that plain,
beyond which, and beyond the sight
of poetry's remembered light,
stand fields of thrice-ripening grain
and orchards heavy with new fruit
hanging above the foamy shore
of deep swirling Ocean. Here,
embraced by this protective moat
and freshened by the scented air
the daughters of the Sea God blow,
are the isles where the blest ones go,

whose perfect peace is Heaven's care.

Now from the plain abrupt before
Orpheus rises the apparition
in bronze and gold of Pluto's mansion,
the massive ever-open door,
the gleam and gloom perceived within.
A moment's breath suspended there,
ever so slight in nether air,
regained at once; he enters in.

The words he sings to the royal pair
enthroned in that resounding room
in filtered paraphrase have come
to us as supposition, bare
of urgency, the ghosts of fact.
He pleads, we're told, invoking Love,
who drove Hell's king to ride above,
to search in sunlight and to abduct
the virgin who now shares his reign,
and justified the unlawful act.
Then, perhaps with greater tact,
the song proceeds in courtly vein:
"Our lives are but on loan from you,
and soon or late you're paid your due.
None from you can hide or flee;
your endless rule's our destiny.
When age by right her life should sever
Eurydice is yours forever.
But by ill chance she's been dragged here
too soon, before her ripening year.
So let the Fates re-weave the thread;
in time again she will be dead.
I only ask for transient hold
on life that must at last grow cold.
But know," — now moving to defiance,
perhaps despairing of compliance —
"Great King, if you refuse my plea
and not release Eurydice,
I will to life return no more.
So both retain or both restore."

Such verses sung to strings it's claimed
"Drew iron tears down Pluto's cheek
and made Hell grant what love did seek."
The might of Death by art was tamed.

Leaving aside this doubtful claim,
whatever the motive or the cause,
the King of Hell relaxed his laws
and put a crown on Orpheus' fame.

The bloodless animation of a shade,
of which a recent perished soul is made,
is barely visible in unlit light
and quivers there in waves of grey and white.
"She's yours to take, but not the way you came:
the narrow path is best, as she is lame.
She'll follow the vibrations of your lyre,
but, lest the terms of this release expire,
in hope of seeing her do not look back
till sunlight shows her emerging from the track."

A hesitation there? No. He thinks best
move on. He's won the object of his quest.

Oh, Orpheus, there's peril in your trust.
Even today in Greece they say the same:
You only leave a house the way you came.

This we remember, and for our sake:
oracular and divine speech,
to prophesy, command or teach,
always leaves wonders in its wake,
the sense and truth for us to make.

So to the narrow path: the colourless
dull slabs that pave this underpass
seem to ingest the fall of feet
and the lyre's harmony and beat.
Faint tremors of the atmosphere,
the silent residue of air,
is all the guidance ghostly sense
can have for life to recommence.
Along this passage underground
all else is memory of sound.
We have been told what happened next,

through hearsay and in written text,
how, reaching sunlight, Orpheus turned
to see her vanished, to Hell returned.
Unthinking or impatient, he
mistook the sun that he could see
for that unseen by Eurydice,
the prototypical mistake
poets are ever like to make.

A line of verse can be erased,
a faulty word or phrase replaced.
Not so an ill-timed turn of the head.
That lives forever with the dead.

What did he see, or not see, in the shadow of the cave?
The final flutter of her ghost? what he had meant to save
disintegrating or sucked back into the vacuum
of Death? Or was she on the instant gone, of which the sum
in time is naught, so that he without time had naught to see?
Or, she within Hell's darkness still, then out in sunlight he
no longer had the means to see the memory of light
of which she was composed. Denied thus to his living sight,
she was not there for him. The act of seeing creates the
    world,
the fact of being non-existent in the underworld.
Or could it simply be she stayed and never followed him?
A solemn trick. And Pluto's warning sealed the stratagem,
for, whether there or not, her presence could not be
    detected.
Nor sound, nor sight, and Pluto's austere purpose is
    effected:
to check the straying man-god, whose mission was to
    celebrate
the transient unity of nature, not to violate its laws.

But Orpheus — we see him there
trying to penetrate with eyes astare
the virtual density of emptiness
where, as with all negation, more is less.
This is the visionary moment when,
as nothing was revealed, he turned again
to where the living world before him spread:
"I, Orpheus, have come back from the dead."

Eurydice's first death he did not mourn,
believing through his art she would return.
But later, Latin poets have him twice
forlorn in grief, unwilling that the price
be paid mortality entails, the second
death the harsher hurt, as what he'd reckoned
through his art, divinity in him,
with hopes all confident, was overcome
by his own frailty. His lyre aside,
forgetful of his art, he crawls to plead
for passage back and rudely is dismissed.
He wails and sobs; for weeks he loiters lost
along the shore, his sorrow and his tears
nourishing his grief. And it appears,
in these accounts, he never does recover,
forgoing all womankind, or as a lover
is unmanned — a sentimental gloss
upon a story of disturbing force
and difficulty, for was it not also said
he simply turned from Hell, with something understood?

V.

The God with vine leaves woven through his hair
leads a train of women wild without care,
by him possessed, the Maenads, and Satyr gangs —
a swarm, with pipes and roarers, hoots and bangs,
chaotically careering through the land,
riotously enforcing his demand
for worship and submission, and killing those
who, for whatever scruple, may reject
the liberty Dionysos does impose.
They feast on beasts, empowered by the God,
ripping apart the living flesh. No "should"
or "would", but "is", entranced with strength ecstatic,
in wake of him where freedom is dogmatic.

Orpheus sings now for a dwindling sect
who worship with him in a place select,
his father's temple. And here fate overtakes.
Here come the Maenads, crowned with living snakes.

They grab the sharp-edged swords stacked up outside,
break in, berserk, and wreak mass homicide.
Orpheus is their particular prey.
His arms and legs they pull and tear away;
with feet braced on his shoulders wrench off his head
and fling it, and his lyre drenched with blood,
into the swirling river.
               It has been said
they floated to the sea, still singing both,
and drifted, as if on a liquid path,
down the Aegean to Lesbos, the lyre to rest
in Apollo's temple, the head an honoured guest
in vine-crowned Dionysos' sacred cave.
The women, when recovered, no longer slave
to their abandonment, and in full sense,
sought in the river Helicon to rinse
their bodies of the man-god's blood, but found
the River God had dived below the ground,
leaving for them the dry and stony bed.
They rolled in pebbly sand and scraped the blood
with sharp-edged stones, as best they could.

The limbs and trunk of Orpheus the Muses, weeping,
searched for and gathered up together for safe-keeping,
and buried them near Mount Olympus by the sea.
The nightingales that nest upon that grave, they say,
sing louder and more sweetly than any on this earth,
announcing to the night air the man-god's rebirth.

Notes

Page 30: *The Annunciation*
This painting is the left panel of the St. Columba Altarpiece
(*c.* 1460) in the Alte Pinakothek, Munich. The centre panel is
The Adoration of the Kings, the right The Presentation in the
Temple. There is another earlier Annunciation, c. 1435, in The
Louvre.

Page 51: *The Moon and Mars in Mani*
Albans
Local term for Albanian migrant workers.

Page 53: *On Blake on a Beach.* The partial quotes are from an
untitled poem in Blake's Notebook Poems, *c.* 1800–1806.

Page 72: *Orpheus IV*
Drew iron tears … love did seek. Milton, Il Penseroso.

Page 74: *Orpheus IV*
He wails and sobs; for weeks he loiters lost
along the shore
Ovid says for seven days (Metamorphoses bk 10), Virgil seven
months (Georgics bk 4). I offer a compromise.